# EASY CLASSICS

## FOR THE YOUNG FLUTE PLAYER

T0056296

Exclusively Distributed By

HAL•LEONARD
CORPORATION
7777 W. BLUEMOUND RD. P.O. BOX 13819 MILWAUKEE, WI 53213

Order Number: CMP 1057-05-400

**EASY CLASSICS FOR THE YOUNG FLUTE PLAYER**
**Flute**

ISBN 90-431-2376-5

CD number: 19-071-3 CMP

# EASY CLASSICS
## FOR THE YOUNG FLUTE PLAYER

**FOREWORD**

EASY CLASSICS FOR THE YOUNG FLUTE PLAYER is a compilation of solo/recital material from the great masters of musical composition that have been specifically arranged for the Beginner through Early Intermediate instrumental soloist. The soloist will find a wide variety of styles and varying levels of difficulty in this book.

This set includes the Piano accompaniment, the Solo part, and a professionally recorded CD that demonstrates each piece. Use these examples to help develop proper performance practices. There is also a recording of the accompaniment alone that can be used for performance (and rehearsal) when a live accompaniment is not available.

# EASY CLASSICS

## FOR THE YOUNG FLUTE PLAYER

# CONTENTS

☐ **Solo with accompaniment**

■ **Accompaniment**

# 1. FANTAISIE IMPROMPTU

Track **2** **3**  Arr. **Ann Lindsay** (ASCAP)

### Jacques Offenbach
# 2. THE CAN-CAN
Arr. **Craig Alan** (ASCAP)

Edward MacDowell

# 3. TO A WILD ROSE

Arr. **James Curnow** (ASCAP)

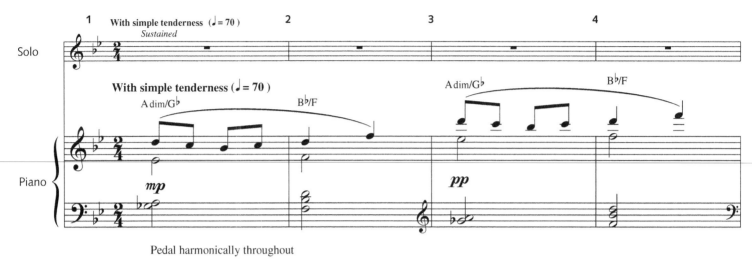
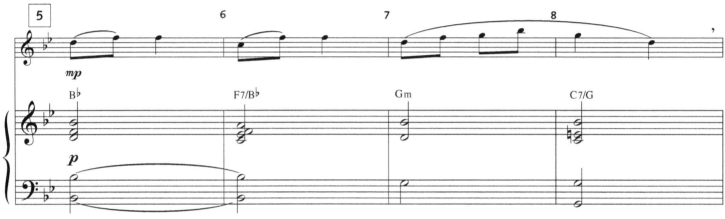
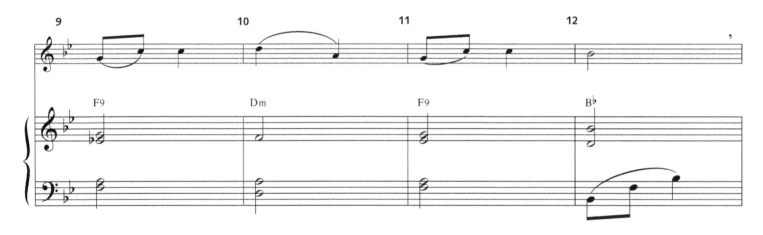
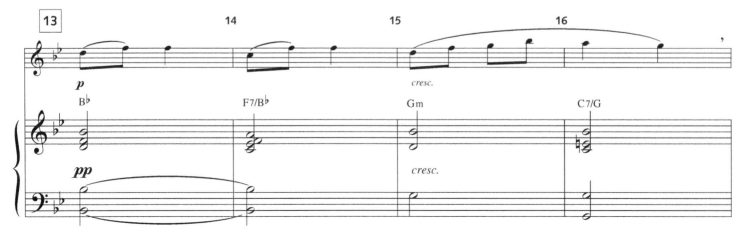

## Johannes Brahms
# 4. HUNGARIAN DANCE # 5

Arr. **James Curnow** (ASCAP)

© 2005 by **Curnow Music Press**

**Julius Benedict**

# 5. THE CARNIVAL OF VENICE

Arr. **Mike Hannickel** (ASCAP)

# 6. AIR from SUITE #3

*"AIR on the G STRING"*

Arr. **Ann Lindsay** (ASCAP)

Track 12 13

# EASY CLASSICS

## FOR THE YOUNG FLUTE PLAYER

**FOREWORD**

EASY CLASSICS FOR THE YOUNG FLUTE PLAYER is a compilation of solo/recital material from the great masters of musical composition that have been specifically arranged for the Beginner through Early Intermediate instrumental soloist. The soloist will find a wide variety of styles and varying levels of difficulty in this book.

This set includes the Piano accompaniment, the Solo part, and a professionally recorded CD that demonstrates each piece. Use these examples to help develop proper performance practices. There is also a recording of the accompaniment alone that can be used for performance (and rehearsal) when a live accompaniment is not available.

# CURNOW®
## MUSIC

EXCLUSIVELY DISTRIBUTED BY

# HAL•LEONARD®
## CORPORATION
7777 W. BLUEMOUND RD. P.O. BOX 13819 MILWAUKEE, WI 53213

# CONTENTS

☐  **Solo with accompaniment**

■  **Accompaniment**

**Frederic Chopin**

# 1. FANTAISIE IMPROMPTU

Arr. **Ann Lindsay** (ASCAP)

Track **2** **3**

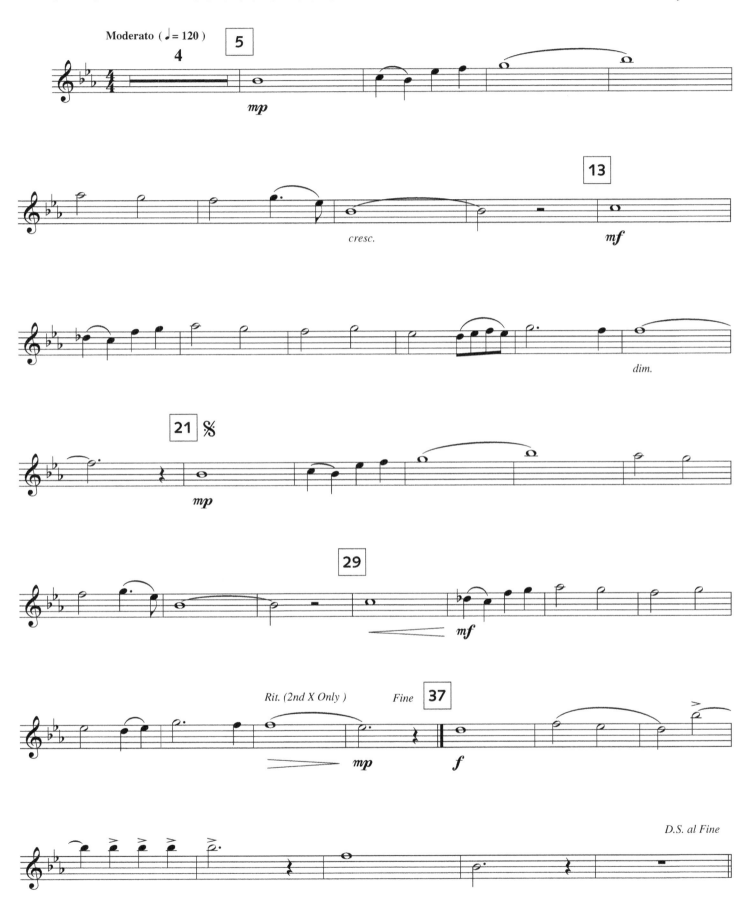

Jacques Offenbach

# 2. THE CAN-CAN

Arr. **Craig Alan** (ASCAP)

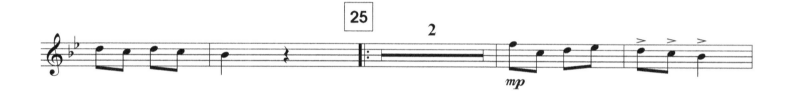

© 2005 by Curnow Music Press, Inc.

Edward MacDowell

# 3. TO A WILD ROSE

Track **6** **7**

Arr. **James Curnow** (ASCAP)

# 4. HUNGARIAN DANCE # 5

Arr. **James Curnow** (ASCAP)

Julius Benedict

# 5. THE CARNIVAL OF VENICE

Track **10** **11**

Arr. **Mike Hannickel** (ASCAP)

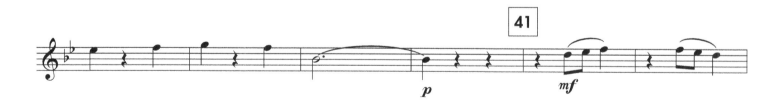

© 2005 by **Curnow Music Press, Inc.**

# 6. AIR from SUITE #3
*"AIR on the G STRING"*

Arr. **Ann Lindsay** (ASCAP)

Victor Herbert
*Fantasy On*
# 7. DAGGER DANCE
from "NATOMA"

Arr. Craig Alan (ASCAP)

Track [14] [15]

Moderato (♩= 124)

# 8. ANDANTE
# from LA CI DAREM LA MANO

*From Don Giovanni*

Arr. **Ann Lindsay** (ASCAP)

W.A. Mozart

# 9. ARIA

from "THE MAGIC FLUTE"

Arr. **Ann Lindsay** (ASCAP)

**Georges Bizet**

# 10. HABANERA

from

## Carmen

Arr. **James Curnow** (ASCAP)

**Jean Joseph Nouret**

# 11. RONDEAU

Arr. **James Curnow** (ASCAP)

Georges Bizet

# 12. TOREADOR'S SONG

from Carmen

Arr. **Mike Hannickel** (ASCAP)

## CLASSICS FOR THE YOUNG FLUTE PLAYER

Music of the great masters: eight wonderful classics in a format that is appropriate for the young instrumentalist: from very easy up to early intermediate levels with a professionally recorded accompaniment CD. Excellent literature for concerts, contests, or home enjoyment. These solos can also be performed with a live band – they are also available as concert band arrangements.

Order Number                    CMP 0543-01-400

## CONCERT SOLOS FOR THE YOUNG FLUTE PLAYER

High quality solo pieces from very easy up to early intermediate levels with a professionally recorded demonstration/accompaniment CD. Features original compositions by some of today's finest composers for a total of twelve outstanding solos in a wide variety of musical styles. Excellent literature for concerts, contests, church, or home enjoyment. Piano accompaniment included.

Order Number                    CMP 1045-05-400

**Victor Herbert**
*Fantasy On*

# 7. DAGGER DANCE

Arr. **Craig Alan** (ASCAP)

from "NATOMA"

W. A. Mozart

# 8. ANDANTE
# from LA CI DAREM LA MANO

*From Don Giovanni*

Arr. **Ann Lindsay** (ASCAP)

# W.A.Mozart
# 9. ARIA
from "THE MAGIC FLUTE"

Arr. **Ann Lindsay** (ASCAP)

### Georges Bizet
# 10. HABANERA
### from
## Carmen

Arr. **James Curnow** (ASCAP)

CMP 1057-05 Flute

Jean Joseph Nouret
# 11. RONDEAU
Arr. **James Curnow** (ASCAP)

RONDEAU: Pg. 3

## Georges Bizet
# 12. TOREADOR'S SONG
### from Carmen

Arr. **Mike Hannickel** (ASCAP)

## CLASSICS FOR THE YOUNG FLUTE PLAYER

Music of the great masters: eight wonderful classics in a format that is appropriate for the young instrumentalist: from very easy up to early intermediate levels with a professionally recorded accompaniment CD. Excellent literature for concerts, contests, or home enjoyment. These solos can also be performed with a live band – they are also available as concert band arrangements.

Order Number                          CMP 0543-01-400

## CONCERT SOLOS FOR THE YOUNG FLUTE PLAYER

High quality solo pieces from very easy up to early intermediate levels with a professionally recorded demonstration/accompaniment CD. Features original compositions by some of today's finest composers for a total of twelve outstanding solos in a wide variety of musical styles. Excellent literature for concerts, contests, church, or home enjoyment. Piano accompaniment included.

Order Number                          CMP 1045-05-400